What Others are Saying About
So Frag & So Bold

"These gems have the precision of A.R. Ammons' short poems, but shimmer with Brown's distinct focus and voice. Handle with equal awareness of the gut-punch and the giggle."

—Abby E. Murray, author of *Hail and Farewell*

"Randy Brown's *So Frag & So Bold* is a delightful assault of poetic playfulness. [...] His poems are micro in composition yet big in heart, posing deep philosophical questions. Ultimately, it takes us where all good poetry should—to consider ourselves, our words, our actions, and the seismic impacts we can have on our shared world."

—Amalie Flynn, author of *Wife and War: The Memoir*

"Often, it is the poet who best enlightens us on war's brutality, its senselessness, and, at times, its peculiar attractiveness. In *So Frag & So Bold*, veteran Randy Brown follows firmly in the footsteps of those war poets [...] A humanizing collection of pithy verses that is worthy of reading and reflection."

— Gregory A. Daddis, author of *Pulp Vietnam: War and Gender in Cold War Men's Adventure Magazines*

"*So Frag & So Bold* is a *tour de force* of wartime poetry, an epic journey through a generation of conflict that seasons the veteran soul with a dash of Wilfred Owen and a pinch of Shel Silverstein."

— Steve Leonard, co-editor of the anthology *To Boldly Go: Leadership, Strategy, and Conflict in the 21st Century and Beyond*

"Crafted with sniper-precision, Randy Brown's lines hit like artillery shells. *So Frag & So Bold* delivers on its title—handle with care!"

— Jason Poudrier, author of *Red Fields*

Other Military-themed Books from Middle West Press LLC

anthologies

Our Best War Stories:
Prize-winning Poetry & Prose
from the Col. Darron L. Wright Memorial Awards
Edited by Christopher Lyke

Why We Write:
Craft Essays on Writing War
Edited by Randy Brown
& Steve Leonard

Reporting for Duty:
U.S. Citizen-Soldier Journalism
from the Afghan Surge, 2010-2011
Edited by Randy Brown

❖   ❖   ❖

poetry collections

Hugging This Rock:
Poems of Earth & Sky, Love & War
by Eric Chandler

Permanent Change of Station and *Forces*
by Lisa Stice

Welcome to FOB Haiku:
War Poetry from Inside the Wire
by Randy Brown, a.k.a. "Charlie Sherpa"

SO FRAG
& SO BOLD

Short Poems, Aphorisms & Other Wartime Fun

Randy Brown
Middle West Press LLC
Johnston, Iowa

So Frag & So Bold
Copyright © 2021 by Randy Brown

❖ ❖ ❖

Poetry / Current Events / Military Life / Humor

*So Frag & So Bold:
Short Poems, Aphorisms & Other Wartime Fun*
by Randy Brown

ISBN (print): 978-1-953665-04-1
ISBN (e-book): 978-1-953665-05-8
Library of Congress Control Number: 2021917804

❖ ❖ ❖

Middle West Press LLC
P.O. Box 1153
Johnston, Iowa 50131-9420
www.middlewestpress.com

❖ ❖ ❖

*Special thanks to James Burns of Aurora, Colorado
and Aramis Calderon of Safety Harbor, Florida
Your patronage helps publish great military-themed writing!*
www.aimingcircle.com

For Sara, Carolyn, and Angie

CONTENTS

first things first

you start off
wanting to change the world;
maybe if you're lucky
you end with a poem

you start off
wanting to write a poem;
maybe if you're lucky
you change the world

how to be a war poet

say you are a poet /
are you not already at war?

Improvised Explosive Thought

any poem is a device
improvised to explode with meaning

the result of
compaction plus combustion

ignited by a trigger

/ word

frag out!

every poet
has a heart filled
with shrapnel

two terminals

any metaphor
is a spark between;

a bridge across
the broken space

what is a koan?

a circular logic
tapering to
a single
point
?

timing

the line between a poem

and a joke

can a poem be

how ? small .

sound of a left-handed football bat, clapping

*"embrace the
Suck."*

*"if you don't mind,
it don't matter."*

*"if it ain't raining,
it ain't training."*

I wonder now at how
it took me so long to figure out:

my drill sergeant
was, in reality, a Buddhist monk.

RANDY BROWN

in the marketplace of ideas

In Iraq, in the book market, stacks remain
unguarded in the street at night.

Iraqis say: *"The reader does not steal;
the thief does not read."*

And yet I hesitate to share my words

here on social media.

daily exercise (haiku)

my morning poems
have begun to sound like Tweets
fragments of bird song

morning prayer

Coffee?

Thank God.

Clausewitzian nature poem

the only thing
war ever changes
is the uniform

a poem

You don't have to make everything
a poem, she said.

Or about
being a Veteran.

"Aliens" (1986)

our first date
was a war movie

Catch-23

If you want peace,
prepare for war.

If you want war,
prepare for war.

the truth is

I know just enough
                  about the Buddha
to be dangerous

I tell my children

to clean their own rooms
to play fair and make right
to always do
the best they can.

And then I apologize
that I am not leaving them
a better world
than my own.

exclamation

What a time to be alive!
What a time to be alive.

What a burden to place upon a single mark
of punctuation.

pauses, for effect

Why, do you hate America?

Why do you hate, America?

a Musing

what do artists call
a group of friends

Jesus texts

I don't care about
who you love

I do care about
who you hate

:)

the urge

sometimes I have to fight
to say I love you
to everyone
I can

no doubt

The world will not end
in my lifetime

but it sure seems hell-bent
on giving it a try

tell me how this ends

what happens when your war
is old enough to enlist?

what happens when your war
is old enough to leave home?

what happens when your war
is old enough to vote?

America

we best reflect

the spaces between us

when we stand

together

uniform of the day (haiku)

Your choice of T-shirt:
Captain America or
(points) "I'm with Stupid"

crossing the line

when you start writing war
as an escape

mode of operation

I don't need to write a great poem,
Just one good enough for now.

I don't need to be a great poet,
Just a serviceable one.

Put enough rounds downrange,
and even the worst shot is bound to hit something.

Just pull the damn trigger.

The New Sherpatudes

If something isn't a threat to life, limb, or eyesight,
maybe it's not such a big deal.

❖   ❖   ❖

Every time an acronym changes,
a Full-Bird gets their wings.

❖   ❖   ❖

Hope is not a Course of Action,
but hate is a tested technique.

❖   ❖   ❖

Everyone has their own war;
no one should have to fight alone.

❖   ❖   ❖

Pride goeth before a fall ...
and/or a change of command.

❖   ❖   ❖

Murphy's Law is a system of systems.

❖   ❖   ❖

The Forever War is a system of systems.

All glory is fleeting. So is technology.

❖ ❖ ❖

"Common Operating Pictures" aren't.

❖ ❖ ❖

You go to Army with the war you have.

❖ ❖ ❖

Indirect fire means never having to say you're sorry.

❖ ❖ ❖

Never communicate more than you know.

❖ ❖ ❖

Never communicate all that you know.

❖ ❖ ❖

The *most-effective* weapon is someone
who doesn't care about getting promoted.

The *most-dangerous* weapon is someone
who cares too much about getting promoted.

❖ ❖ ❖

When you're a hammer, everything looks like a nail.
When you're out on patrol, everything looks like an I.E.D.

When life gives you lessons, "make lesson-ade."

❖   ❖   ❖

Never brief half-baked Courses-of-Action.
The commander will invariably select the one
you meant as a joke.

❖   ❖   ❖

Everyone can tell you why they're going to war,
but few can say why they went.

❖   ❖   ❖

War is hell; hell is other people.

❖   ❖   ❖

"All this has happened before;
all this will happen again."

❖   ❖   ❖

Nostalgia is a disease, suffered by old soldiers.

The Golden Sherpatude

never hit "send"
without first asking
whether one's words
have the potential
to improve lives.

RANDY BROWN

leadership (a.k.a. "mission command")

the most-potent mojo
is the ability to trust

they'll know when
to wake you up

a quiet professional professes through haiku

1.
A practice of war
involves daily sacrifice.
The job is a trade.

2.
This we will defend:
Constitution, people, land.
(The order matters.)

3.
Any rag-bag Joe
who ever raised their right hand?
Now also, my kin.

4.
The only glory
one should seek is the respect
of one's own soldiers.

5.
"Secret" means secret.
Loose lips sink ships, lives, careers.
Keep your big trap shut.

6.
Your moral compass
should be red-light readable
for work in the dark.

7.
Share knowledge freely.
A lesson-learned is like cheap
immortality.

break, break, break

any poem is a communications tool;
the instructions are embedded as code

punctuation and line breaks
encrypt and specify

how it must be read
but not (necessarily) what it means

think of it
as "Push-To-Talk"

like a radio
for the mind

just-another-day haiku

Anyone know why
flags are at half-staff again?
Second time this month.

Armistice Day haiku

Eleventh hour.
Eleventh day and month.
Wish that peace could last.

chance encounters

I first met the Buddha
in a comic book.

I see Jesus every day
on social media.

Muhammad is
my next-door neighbor.

Mindfulness, empathy, and wonder
take practice

but we must also
take opportunities.

blind men & veterans

we each describe
                    seeing the elephant

differently

is it, a poem

is it a poem

is it still a poem
if I didn't change it

is it still a poem
if I didn't unpack it

is it still a poem
if I didn't complicate it

is it still a poem
if I didn't break it

is it still a poem
if I didn't fix it

is it still a poem

is it

rounds complete

the mortars suck
the mortars wait
the mortars rouse

the mortars
                        hang
        then shoot
        and shoot
        and shoot
        and shoot

the mortars pause
the mortars wait

the mortars play Spades
the mortars wait

the mortars wait
the mortars wait

the mortars suck

RANDY BROWN

who-knew (haiku)

who I am depends
on who you are, where we are,
and who's buying drinks.

a sliding scale of difficulties

strategic miscalculation

                        operational cock-up

tactical error

                        sharp end of the stick

wrong place, wrong time

                        this really happened

guess you had to be there

                        wish you were here

Most Likely /
Most Dangerous Enemy Courses of Action

what "Most" /
threatens my children

social media /
unending war

the rat race /
the daily grind

half-baked policies /
climate change

a lack of hope /
a lack of justice

my constant distraction /
my constant distraction

the stand

if you can't stand injustice
take a knee

if you pray for others
take a knee

if you believe in freedom, not fabric
let others see

you practice
what you preach

on war poetry

we write the war /
the war writes us

even the ones
who got away clean

Winchester

are we done
when we fire

nothing but
blank sheets

being & becoming

metaphors
            are created

in the space between

trust me

we are all pretending

about everything

RANDY BROWN

your past is prologue

we are each >

what we remember

This is Just to "Say Again All After ..."

After William Carlos Williams' "This Is Just to Say"

I have expended
the pineapples
that were in
the ammo box

and which
you were probably
saving
for final protective fires

Forgive me
they were explosive
so frag
and so bold

RANDY BROWN

breaking news

so much depends
on a broken line

and the resulting alterations
of space

and meaning

reminders

1.
first, do no harm.

2.
love one another.

3.
give yourself permission.

4.
make mistakes &
learn from them.

5.
we'll always have
the Alamo.

defensive driver

I never understood
why some Joes startled
at every blowing grocery bag
until I came home myself
and found the camels hiding

in cornfields

behind bridges

everywhere

How to End a War Story

(According to Thucydides)

Step 1. Go to Ephesus
Step 2. Offer sacrifice to Artemis
Step 3. ???????

all this will be yours:

"all this
has happened before"

&

"all this
will happen again"

ACKNOWLEDGEMENTS

My desktop is scatter-filled with sticky-notes and fortune-cookie receipts. Many of the word- and line-experiments in this chapbook seem too slight to warrant serious consideration by serious literary journals. Still, I've been lucky to find a few fellow travelers who not only accepted and published such work, but encouraged more of it.

I am grateful to the editors of the following magazines and journals, in which some of these poems first appeared—some in slightly different versions:

"**Clausewitzian nature poem**" first appeared in *Collateral Journal* issue No. 4.2 in Spring 2020

"**daily exercise**" first appeared in *The Wrath-Bearing Tree* July 2020

"**I tell my children**" first appeared in *The Wrath-Bearing Tree* July 2020

"**just another day haiku**" first appeared in *Collateral Journal* issue No. 4.2 in Spring 2020

"**morning prayer**" first appeared in *Collateral Journal* issue No. 4.2 in Spring 2020

"**Most Likely / Most Dangerous Enemy Course of Action**" first appeared in *The Wrath-Bearing Tree* October 2018

"**a poem**" first appeared in *Collateral Journal* issue No. 4.2 in Spring 2020

"**a quiet professional professes through haiku**" first appeared Jan. 24, 2017 on Tom Ricks' "Best Defense" blog, which was hosted on the

Foreign Policy magazine website. The set of haiku was a response to Ricks' call for 150-word micro-essays regarding the question, "What should a military professional profess?"

"the stand" first appeared in *The Wrath-Bearing Tree* October 2018

"tell me how this ends" first appeared in *Collateral Journal* No. 3.1 in November 2018

"This is Just to 'Say All Again After ...'" first appeared in *The Wrath-Bearing Tree* October 2018

NOTES

Readers of my first collection, *Welcome to FOB Haiku: War Poems from Inside the Wire*, may remember my regular use of 5-7-5 haiku—the "official" kind that many people first encounter in grade school—to illuminate aspects of military life. Tell someone a poem is a haiku, and even the most-rabid self-described poetry non-reader will usually stop to count the syllables.

I hope that *So Frag & So Bold* might be accessible in similar ways. Call something a poem? Sure, if that gets you to read it. Call it something a joke or a riddle or a puzzle? That works, too.

It's OK to laugh at my words—indeed, that is my intent—but I also hope readers will detect something more at work than just witty wordplay. In short, I would love for these type-filled gadgets to ignite questions … confusions … conversations … connections. *Enjoy!*

"all this will be yours": This poem evokes the religious concept of eternal return—and echoes a catchphase from the 2004-2009 television series *Battlestar Galactica*. I also quote it in "The New Sherpatudes."

"Armistice Day haiku": The original Armistice Day (Nov. 11, 1918) marked the end of World War I. The initial document ending the war became effective on the eleventh hour on the eleventh day of the eleventh month. In the United States, November 11th is also Veterans Day. Elsewhere, it is celebrated as Remembrance Day.

"America": This poem was written during the COVID-19 pandemic, when wearing face masks and maintaining social distances were recommended techniques to mitigate transmission of disease.

"blind men & veterans": This poem evokes both the ancient Indian parable of the blind men and the elephant, as well as the 19th century American idiom "seeing the elephant." The latter refers to gaining experience at the cost of disillusionment. In military contexts, "seeing the elephant" meant the experience of combat.

"Clausewitzian nature poem": The military strategy writer Carl von Clausewitz (1780-1831) argued that while the essential nature of war does not change—it is always violent and political—characteristics such as tactics and technology change from era to era.

"The Golden Sherpatude": This unnumbered maxim (see also "The New Sherpatudes") lent itself to presentation as a poem.

"Most Likely / Most Dangerous Enemy Course of Action": In analyzing battle plans, military intelligence staffers are often called upon to identify for their commanders two predictions: a "most-likely [enemy] course of action" (MLCOA) and a "most-dangerous [enemy] course of action" (MDCOA). The former is the way an enemy is thought likely to attack, based upon an understanding of their doctrine, tactics, and behaviors in the field. The latter is the course-of-action that could most-prevent friendly forces from achieving their objectives.

"the stand" was written in response to critics of those who, inspired by the example of former San Francisco 49ers quarterback Colin Kaepernick, seek to call attention to racial injustices by taking a knee during sporting-event ceremonies. In the military, "take a knee" can be an informal way to say "take a moment to rest and recover." Taking a knee is also variously used as a technique to put soldiers in a short halt for instruction or rest, and to indicate non-hostile intent to a crowd.

"a quiet professional professes through haiku" was originally written in response to journalist Tom Ricks' call for 150-word micro-essays regarding the question, "What should a military professional profess?" The haiku first appeared Jan. 24, 2017 on Tom Ricks' "Best Defense" blog, which was hosted on the *Foreign Policy* magazine website.

"This is Just to 'Say Again All After ...'" The poetry of American Imagist poet William Carlos Williams (1883-1963), including most notably his 1934 poem "This is Just to Say," lends itself to satiric mimicry on social media. My version exchanges "plums" for "pineapples" (hand grenades), and changes "so sweet / and so cold" to "so frag / and so bold." I like to imagine the lines read in the voice of the Shiba Inu "doge" meme on the Internet: "So frag! Much bold!"

The phrase "Say Again" is a radio-telephone procedural phrase, when the caller requests all or part of a transmission to be repeated.

"tell me how this ends" refers to a quote by retired U.S. Army general officer David A. Petraeus. It was originally spoken to Rick Atkinson during a 2003 interview, when Petraeus was a major general and commander of the 101st Airborne Division in Iraq. It is also the title of a 2008 biography of Petraeus, written by Linda Robinson.

"leadership (a.k.a. 'mission command')": In U.S. military doctrine, the concept of "Mission Command" involves empowering subordinates to make decisions and take actions based on mission objectives, rather than explicit permissions or instructions. Within such contexts, commanders sometimes set "wake-up" criteria—conditions, reports, or news at which they wish to be immediately awakened and informed.

"The New Sherpatudes": Blogging as "Charlie Sherpa," I first published a set of 26 numbered "Sherpatudes" in 2012. These maxims describe how to conduct oneself in a Tactical Operations Center (TOC), and in life. (Example: "No. 10: 'Digital trumps analog, until you run out of batteries.'") The originals were also published in *Welcome to FOB Haiku.*

"Winchester": In military jargon and radio procedure, the brevity code "Winchester" is called when a unit has expended all ordnance.

"How to End a War Story": In his *History of the Peloponnesian War,* oft studied in modern military professional circles, Athenian historian and general Thucydides (460-400 BCE) ends on an unfinished sentence. I find this at turns sad, meaningful, and hilarious.

The 3-step structure of this poem is informed by the profit-seeking underpants gnomes of TV's "South Park," season 2, episode 17.

THANKS

To quote *1 Corinthians 10, verse 31*: "So whether you eat or drink or whatever you do, do it all for the glory of God" (NIV). I pray that includes journalism, puns, and snarky war poetry.

Thanks to my wife and my children, who daily wake me to possibility.

Thanks to Sara Anderson, Carolyn Jacobson, and Angie Hoth, to whom this chapbook is dedicated. To quote former *Chicago Tribune* columnist Mary Schmich: "Understand that friends come and go, but with a precious few you should hold on. Work hard to bridge the gaps in geography and lifestyle, because the older you get, the more you need the people who knew you when you were young."

Thanks to Gregory A. Daddis, director at the Center for War and Society at San Diego State University, and author most recently of *Pulp Vietnam: War and Gender in Cold War Men's Adventure Magazines*. Daddis graciously laughed at "Clausewitzian nature poem"—but took me seriously when I asked if he'd consider endorsing this chapbook.

Thanks to war poet Amalie Flynn *(Wife and War: The Memoir)*, for her constant and constructive interrogations, through her curations of visual art and poetry, of the world we make together. Flynn is the poetry editor at *The Wrath-Bearing Tree*, which I highly recommend to both readers and writers. I also eagerly anticipate her forthcoming *September Eleventh*, an epic poem presented in fragments.

Thanks to my occasional editorial co-conspirator Steve Leonard, a.k.a. "Doctrine Man," whose explorations of pop culture, business writing, and military strategy now span 5-year missions, fantastic kingdoms, and galactic empires. I have promised him a future poem about Star Fleet Battles. In the meantime, make sure to check out *To Boldly Go: Leadership, Strategy, and Conflict in the 21st Century and Beyond*.

Thanks to war poet Jason Poudrier *(Red Fields)*, whose inspiration, wisdom, and advice continues to resonate in my life and writing, years after our first conversations at Military Experience & the Arts conferences. I am also forever mindful of the "What's Up, Doc?" voice of his poem "Artillery Kill":

> *I flipped a switch*
> *the rocket launched*
> *and landed with an*
> *ACME cartoon cloud [...]*

Thanks to war poet Abby E. Murray, founding editor at *The Collateral Journal,* and author of the poetry books *Hail and Farewell, How to Be Married after Iraq,* and *Quick Draw: Poems from a Soldier's Wife.* I owe Murray many poetic debts, not the least of which was helping stick a label on what I had previously regarded as only scraps and fragments. *I'll take "What is a koan?" for $200, please, Alex?*

And, finally, thanks to my fellow practitioners and patrons of military-themed writing at The Aiming Circle (www.aimingcircle.com), and my colleagues at the Military Writers Guild. *"Keep writing!"* and *"Attack! Attack! Attack!"*

ABOUT THE WRITER

Randy Brown traveled the world as part of an active-duty U.S. Air Force family in the 1970s, then landed permanently and happily in the American Midwest. A former editor of community and metro newspapers, as well as national trade and consumer magazines, he is now a freelance writer and editor based in Central Iowa.

Brown embedded with his former Iowa Army National Guard unit as a civilian journalist in Afghanistan, May-June 2011. A 20-year military veteran with one overseas deployment, he subsequently authored the award-winning 2015 collection *Welcome to FOB Haiku: War Poems from Inside the Wire.*

His poetry and essays have appeared widely in print and on-line, as well as anthologies. He even appeared as an "on screen" character in the 2021 *True War Stories* anthology from Z2 Comics, Denver.

Brown is a three-time poetry finalist in the Col. Darron L. Wright Memorial Writing Awards. He co-edited the 2019 Military Writers Guild anthology *Why We Write: Craft Essays on Writing War*, and curated the 2015 project *Reporting for Duty: U.S. Citizen-Soldier Journalism from the Afghan Surge, 2010-2011.*

Brown was the winner of the 2018 "Untold Stories" poetry contest administered by *Flyover: Journal of Writing & the Environment*. He was the winner of the inaugural Madigan Award for humorous military-themed writing, presented in 2015 by Negative Capability Press, Mobile, Alabama.

He is the current poetry editor at the literary journal *As You Were*, published twice a year by the non-profit Military Experience & the Arts. He is also a member of Military Reporters & Editors, the Military Writers Guild, and the Military Writers Society of America.

As "Charlie Sherpa," he writes about modern war poetry at: www.fobhaiku.com; and military writing at: www.aimingcircle.org.

Follow him on Twitter: @FOB_haiku

DID YOU ENJOY THIS BOOK?

Tell your friends and family about it, or post your thoughts via social media sites, like Facebook and Twitter! On-line communities that serve military families, veterans, and service members are also ideal places to help spread the word about this book, and others like it!

You can also share a quick review on websites for other readers, such as Goodreads.com. Or offer a few of your impressions on bookseller websites, such as Amazon.com and BarnesandNoble.com!

Better yet, recommend the title to your favorite local librarian, poetry society or book club leader, museum gift store manager, or independent bookseller! There is nothing more powerful in business of publishing than a shared review or recommendation from a friend.

We appreciate your support! We'll continue to look for new stories and voices to share with our readers. Keep in touch!

You can write us at:

Middle West Press LLC
P.O. Box 1153
Johnston, Iowa 50131-9420

Or visit: www.middlewestpress.com

❖   ❖   ❖

Other poetry collections from Middle West Press LLC:

Welcome to FOB Haiku:
War Poetry from Inside the Wire,
by Randy Brown, a.k.a. "Charlie Sherpa"

Permanent Change of Station and *Forces*
by Lisa Stice

www.ingramcontent.com/pod-product-compliance
Lightning Source LLC
Chambersburg PA
CBHW032212040426
42449CB00005B/556